UNFINISHED SYMPHONY

For Sue-Ellen, Seamus, Liz, Sam, Goldie, Kelsie, Buster, Fat Cat and Walter

The Drive

I did not ride to warn the British are coming.
Nor did I drive Le Mans in the rain.
No pony express.
No message to Garcia.
But I drove 101 through hell and high water to Yarmouth

And survived the rain.

Not much chance for heroics these days.
No beaches to storm.
No bombers to arm.
No maidens to save.
But I conquered the worst new Scotland Has

to offer.

And I drove like Paul Revere on a mission

Or like McClaren in the rain.

JAZZ MASTER CLASS

The world gets better in little ways
The events are different
But the people are always the same. These
are the thoughts that the Jazz master
Proposed.
Before he blew his horn.
Sweet and sour notes of
Profound humanity
All on a Chautauqua morn.

Doggie Dreams

Doggies have great fun Biting

chewing shaking Doggie toys.

Elk horns are tough
Clean teeth provide Hours

of chewing.

Tennis balls are
Fun to chase
And grab from your hand.
Soft chewies are adored
But soon leak fluffy
White stuff on the floor.
Easy for doggies to do
But when you try to stuff
White fluffy stuff
Into your chewie
It is so difficult and
Sewing it closed
Is a pain in the fingers.
I wonder if friendships Are

like that.

Fun to play with
Hard to put back together.

BUSTER

He waits for his mama Under

the dining table

Eyes piercing the door
A groan here
A whine there
Now up and changing direction
To stare at the other door
Oh where oh where
Is my mama tonight I am so

tired of this old man I could

bite his fat hand.

RODNEY THE BASTARD

RODNEY TURNER, YOU BASTARD YOU.
You know of course I am at least 50 percent Irish

 And we never forget our grudges.

You tormented me out of Troop 14
Called me a fat little shit
Put my bike in the sewer It

was never the same.

One thing you did not know Rodney Turner
How I could be six feet and 200 pounds
 At 15.
Oh, I got my revenge some 60 years ago
Behind the Highland Avenue movie house.
I grew, and you did not
Pounded your ass in front of your friends.
And now we are old and

still hanging around

 I have a message for

you.
Thank you, Rodney Turner,
And bless you Rodney Turner
For Helping me to grow in other ways.
Without you I would never understand

Be open to and receptive to my black and gay friends.
How would I have any idea of the depths of despair
That drives hands up don't shoot
The comes out of horns of the blues.
How could I have felt the nausea
Of a return to academic anti- Semitism?
So, Rodney Turner, thank you for helping me
To hear the silence between the words
And bless you for helping me grasp the whistle walk.
Bless you Rodney Turner, you bastard you.

DEAR DETROIT

I hate you.
I love you.
You piss me off.
You brought me pleasure.
You are the pinnacle of corruption.

You are the symbol of hard muscle never giving up.
You are the aroma of punchkies on the way to work.
You are the fear of stopping at red lights at night.
You are the roar of Lions, Tigers, Red Wings.
You are the oh so honest Police chief
with 100 dollar bills falling from his ceiling.
You are brave and brilliant and artistic.
You are selfish and stupid.
Detroit, you are my old home
Middle America, the promise of rebirth.
Detroit, I can't stop loving you Although

I keep trying.

BUSTER

He waits for his mama
Under the dining table
Eyes piercing the door
A groan here
A whine there
Now up and changing direction
To stare at the other door
Oh where oh where
Is my mama tonight I am so

tired of this old man I could

bite his fat hand.

MY DA

Like the song said
My da was a rolling stone
He found other things to do Than
play with me or you. My brother
missed him more than me Said he
would always faithful be.
But now he has gone and died
And left me to be the one who tried
To be the Da he would never be.

ANCIEN REGIME

Emptying the trash can
A piece of paper escaped
To the floor. A picture
Of a lighthouse on one
side
An empty calendar on the other.

Once there were calendars to
rule my life. Be here.
Be there. Be two, no three places at once.
First class seats
Chauffeured limos
WSJ and bottled water in back

And sizzling steaks

Requiring mountains of Pepcids

Today my calendar has no writing

On this date or that date or any date.

Now I need not take TUMS Or

feel the burnt heat.

While I used to curse the darkened calendar,

Now I curse the light.

DEAR DR. SPONG

(After six lectures by Bishop John Spong, noted author and Bishop of the Episcopal Church)

Now what?
73 years it took me
Through Roman Catholicism
Greek Orthodox, Methodist, Buddhism
4 Years high Anglican 7 times a week
Incense even, serving at the altar,

Then Zen meditation, Republican moderation, Atheist
agnostic and finally swallowing my pride Presbyterian
- Da rolling over in his grave.
First Church I ever joined voluntarily.

And now you.
Great stuff your daily messages.
Us aged love it. We crowd around
Sitting in the rain
While you preach deconstruction, Intelligence
and, with the fervor of evangelism, Common
sense.
Great stuff in deed.
But what are we to do now?

No pearly gates. No wise Peter at the door.
No forgiveness of sins. No great
white father to comfort us Now at
the hour of our death.
Where is the Peace?
Where is the choir of angels?
Where is my opiate of the people?
What are we to do now
That we no longer can cling To
our guns and Bibles?

Dr. Spong you had to go
And wrench me back to my Stubborn

humanism and the religion Of the

Golden Rule.

Now at the hour of my death I

have only my own score sheet of

Good and Evil. Better balance the

books, wouldn't you say?

An Alamo Scout in Hollywood

My boss was a tough nut
Brilliant in his way
Made 14 movies Made

money on all but one and

broke even on that.

On the Paramount lot
Everyone knew

Don't piss off Chuck
He's one you don't want to screw.
NBC would pay us plenty
To remake Hogan's Heroes
But put a stinker in the contract.

Chuck picked up the script
And without a word
Left the network stooges to
play with their parts. He was
a good man I thought, And I
learned a lot. A young man
in a top indie Movie
company, well fine.

One thing gave me pause.
Prejudice is ugly. And Chuck
Hated the Japanese. This was not good
Because the company needed selling And
the Japanese were willing.

I knew Chuck had fought the Japanese
In the jungles of the Philippines
Rescuing prisoners not burned alive.
But I thought I would make one last try.

Chuck, I said, the war is over

And the money is good and
Don't you think prejudice should not kill the sale.
He said, I can't stand the smell of them.
I shrugged and said Chuck this is a good deal.
And besides, you can't smell them.

His back to the front door, He smiled and said,
Well, three of them just walked in the door.
And of course, they did. And the most
profitable movie company Is no more.

CRACKERS, ATLANTA 1952

CooooooooooColaaaaa

CooooooooooColaaaaa

Getcha coledriks heah.

Black people over there in the Nigra bleachers
Sign boards surrounding the field backed by a fence
With a discrete hole for adventurous kids, later

a Sears replaced Ponce de Leon Park (It's gone

too now.).

The warm salty aroma of popcorn, peanuts and

cotton candy.

The lineup tonight,
Ebba St Clair behind the plate
The soon to be great Eddie Mathews at third
Gene Verble at shortstop
Frank Torre at first (yeah, that one)
Bob Thorpe in left

Harry Hannebrink (amazing wide stance)in right
And the amazing Ralph Country Brown Whose

wife would not let him move to the majors

Patrolling center.

Pitching tonight, Art Fowler.
Pitching coach, Whitlow Wyatt
(Death by suicide)
And the super racist former star Dixie

Walker managing.

Nat Peeples, a black man
Who opened a slot for Henry Aaron later, on the bench
Walker fired for resisting Hammering Hank and

Wyatt gets his chance.

And Hugh Casey warming up in the bullpen.

Getcha Coledrinks heah.

Pencil ready
Discarded scorecard marked for recording
Safely ensconced after sneaking through the hole
Discretely. Later caught by owner
Earl Mann who surprised me
Offering to let me be a temporary ball boy.
Mama said no cause of undesirable people.

Getch Coledrinks heah
Peanuts popcorn Crackerjacks
CooooColaaaaa
CoooookeColaaaa.

All this floating in my head
After meeting two detectives
At the bar of a NY bistro talking baseball
And waiting for the Wall Street Journal guy
To buy lunch. Bragged I could
Recite the 1952 lineup of the Atlanta Crackers.

Black detective punches white detective
And loudly exclaims, Crackers!
"Crackers!" You got to be kidding,
Laughing and punching the detective with his beer

They couldn't call them that, Could they? Could they?
Atlanta fucking **_Crackers_**!
He laughed and laughed
And never noticed I forgot The

second baseman.

St. P Day

I watched the young girl
In dark coat, dark eyes,
and
Curly dark hair today.

She wore curly, green,
make-believe Flowers.
  And stood with friends.

Her eyes spit laughter and,
Sometimes disapproving
And pointing out
Faux pas, the plural.

You see,
 she was an expert on St. P. Day Parades,
Having several terms
With St. Anne and St. Jo
I watched closely, quite closely,
Too closely, I'm afraid, to see
If she said, *"oh my,"* or *"oh dear,"*
Or *"my, but Parnell's dead and gone."*

Each, one of
the one's who'd
been But a line:
 but always ready to die.

I snorted, myself, and shrugged
What kind does it take?
To keep this silly tune humming?
 What blither! What blah!

After a bit I kept tabs
On a stout, short man who'd tip his cap Every
Time Old Glory would pass.
 Not a grand gesture. Just enough.
I thought, now here's a man
Who'd know the likes of
Danny O', Wolfe Toen,
Emmett, Pearse, Fitzpatrick.

Each, one of the
one's who'd
been but a line:
 but always ready to die.

I figured, calculated, I'd say,
Hah, he's drunk or figuring or Calculating
to be a character in some Flick.

Then, the Hibernians slumped past in
Large Italian looking haircuts, black
Wash 'n wear trench coats.
(surely one revolver among them) ***Each,***
one of the one's who'd been but a
line:
 but always ready to die.

And then the skirl of pipes.
I had no hat to tip for Old Glory
And so I stood straight for the
skirl.

And then, after a while,
With the sun on my cheek
And the wind, cold, at my back, I
looked at the girl again.

  She was Young
and she was pretty.
And I smiled this time.

So she smiled before
I had to go Up the
elevator.
And straighter I stood.

Walking quickly,
after that,
Quickly through the dark young
Girls (Black Irish, I suppose)

Each, one of the
one's who'd
been but a line:
 but always ready to die.

And thin young men
(and their Clearasil), Thinking
about lifting my feet clicking
my heels.

Walking to the din the
humming,
 the roll, and the clang of
McNamara's Band.

Each, one of
the one's who'd
been but a line:
 but always ready to die.

1967, 2010

YEATS COMPLAINT.

Dear Professor Jack:
class cancelled

 For I know not
what lack--do know

God, Himself, does not love
Irish poetry.

He, Himself, places whiskey at
the poet's hand.

Blame not the weatherman
who pours this misery

Blame, instead, the Almighty
Who thwarts Heaney

Who tortures the likes of Willis and
people like me?

 Because God himself does not love Irish
poetry.

Your faithful servant and
savant to be

sending silly poetry (bump) to
thee. (thump)

Business Class

My salad days in Hong Kong
Found broccoli trees
 Like mushrooms Chopped
This way and that way
In squares, rounds, boxes,
NEC, Kent and Camel
Splashed in a bowl
Between Center and Kowloon
Poured down the peak A
salad dressing of garlic
And sweat.

On the water music in Sydney
Past the Opera House
With extended wings we fly.
The boom sends back Reggae beats
to Koala bear screams and we fly.
The red hot unfiltered sun
Soaks through the 15 salve

Infiltrating our backs While
we fly.

In Honolulu mama
We have done the hookey lau
The hookey lau
(You were laughing)
Eating poi
And drinking large vats of rum juice
(You were pointing)
Under orange skies
While earnest young faces
Mouth ????s
On a local and a global basis.
(You were watching)
I saw you there
Doing the hooky lau
The hook lau too.

In the Frankfort follies
Halls and halls and halls
Of wheels
Pointed up and out
Dreamed up by little men
In white coats and jackets.
Each year the sheet metal
Rusts a little sooner

Until
One day a dot
Of brown falls upon
A sheet of blue
And then we know
We've driven too far.

On my Magyar holiday
Upon the rim of the highest hill
In Buda
The sun drips down behind a higher hill
As we run between small singing girls
Climbing big guns ringing the war museum.
Lovers kiss
Boys play chess
And you and I
Find the night sky in Budapest.

On a direct shot from Messe
We bounced and skidded into Toronto
Making a right turn at Windsor
Where border guards carried no machine guns And
merely waved us through.
All of our lies went untold
How two lovers rounded the earth
And moved on to Detroit one night.

2010

A SEASON IN NEW YORK

Beside the peanut vendor
In Central Park
The carousel played
And children larked,
And there by the zoo
And on to the mall,
We held hands and knew
One touch of spring.

Upon the rim of the sky
We sat silent,
Made still by our desire,
And watched the moon make
Love to the river.
And you said:
"The statue of Liberty
Looks out across the water
And into the sky."

There was that one fine day on the water

You and I and the young married couple,
Your old friends and now mine, under the sun
With a thermos of drinks, feeling the waves.
She spoke languidly, your friend's young wife, of time
And how its imminence was upon us
And how we can never really be prepared
To be thrust out into the world.

He laughed and poured another round
And then started the engines once again.
Gather ye rosebuds, he laughed,
Today, for it may rain another day.

And you smiled—I saw your burn and offered
My shirt but you declined and we all laughed
For you eventually took it.
I thought you would speak, but you only smiled,

And there in the heat that one summer's day
With our friends there, his hand upon his drink,
Hers making shallow waves, you smiled, and I felt
The constant dread of fleeting things upon me.

You gesture gracefully
Yet with an acknowledged strength
Holding my every breath
Between the fingers of your hands:
"All the old grey hairs
Are like the sun's rays at dark—

Once I had long hair
And my feet were not bound by shoes
And rings adorning my fingers
Were more likely to be daisies
Than of silver or gold
And my prince was of the earth
And held grapes between his fingers…"
All night we talk on, you and I,
Of politics and nations
Or even of you and I,
Your head inclined as you speak:
"But what shall we speak of
When we are old, when
December's roaring blast precedes
The real cold---And what
Loves shall we moan for
And what wars?"
And though you follow my every gesture
With tender regard,
You take care we never touch.

We stood by the fountain at the Plaza
And waited silently for you to go:
Snowflakes began to whisper about us.
And our dark coats admitted the cold.
I did not speak—there were no words
Until, by the fountain at the Plaza,
You asked, "Will I see you again?"
And I answered, "Yes, in the spring."

"When the frost melts," you called.
"Yes," I returned, "and when the waters run."

In my quiet room
I wait upon my couch, Close to the door,
For the sound of an idling engine
Or the slamming of a taxi door,
Perhaps the whirr of the elevator
Or a shoe upon the floor---
Some sign that you have come home.

New York City, March 1963

THEME SONG

Alan, you bastard, you.

I'd rather see the world through horned rim glasses
Than blow my cool like you have.

We started out with you, howling
Holy Holy Holy.

You seemed on top of everything Unholy.
You seemed to know.

And when you screamed, fuck you America America,
You screamed for us. But, somewhere along the way,
You fucked up, fucked yourself, Alan.

You let them put you on a subway poster,
Dubbed in Uncle Sam clothes, crying out for
Some commercial Underground Generation.

Better you should espouse Gillette.

We wanted you to grow up with us. Speak for us,
Go on from Holy Holy Holy to things Unholy. To jump,
With us, upon the shrieking, lying throats.

Instead, you're content to pull the chains of three score old men
In their great white wigs regaling them of your long road of
Hallucinations, and how cool it was, man.

Instead, you are compelled to tell red eyed cameras
About your masturbations and how your arms swelled with pride.

You let your face go fuzzy until
We could see it no longer.

And then you were no longer on top of things Unholy.

You were leaving us to go our own way while you
Cavorted with Timothy.

You let us forget you Alan, except as that funny old man
With a beard and a story.

Bruce runs a newspaper. Ed investigates Aeneas. Sean has his
Typewriter. Meanwhile, Alan, back at the lBJ ranch, is playing the fool.

There was a time, Alan, when you could have been Walt, Baby. You
Could have bared your chest, your phlegmatic chest, to the sky and cried,
I am You. You are me. Let us begin.

Instead, Alan, you are Bobby Benson. You are the B-Bar-B Riders.
Jack Armstrong. Sam Spade. The Green, bless him, Hornet. You are a
thousand restless early afternoons and evenings. You are
You are, in short, now, a fool.

I am sorry for that Alan. We are all sorry for that Alan.
We thought you had it in you to be a hero. But you would
Rather play the fool. Pull your pud. Put the old men on. Scare
The old ladies.

You could have been so much more.

You could have said, in '54,
Ho Chi wears a white hat and rides
A white horse.

You could have made a modest proposal to eat
Black flesh, as the most humane of actions.

You could have ignited the Star of David
Before a Baptist Church.

You could have drawn Richard Nixon in
An old pair of shoes.

Fought a war.

Raised a roof.

Found a cause.

Been, would you believe, a poet.

You know all the words, Alan. And
All the rhymes.

But you chose to carry the burden of fool, an
Albatross. You chose, instead, to grab us by the lapels
And, with one mad eye, tell your foolish story one time too many.

Alan, you could have done more.

Alan, you could have gained respect without giving in to the Maltese
Crossed, Black Jackets and fuzzy faces. You could have told those old
men

In their white wigs that you and we can have different ideas without
Being an old fool saddled with a large bird.

You do not talk for us, Alan. You do not speak for us.

Alan, you bastard you.
1968

SABBATH SCENE

We laughed
Away our griefs on queer formed freaks
And shot
Animal eyes and human thighs
And dared
Our roller-coaster eyes to scream
And loved
Beneath the sweating summer scenes
At Coney.

New York City
1961

The Edge

Seated upon
A pale-yellow sky
In February a little boy
Bouncing ball fallen.

Splashing tears. Screaming,
It was a hurricane, it was
A hurricane, mommy, that
Blew me down.

Nonsense. November. Or
September. Or between.
But not in February.

Now let me patch your knee my child
And then I think you'd best take a restful nap.

Laid out against a cloud
His knee supported by two
Sculptured triton hews,
A little child cannot see
A pale-yellow sky.

Dry. Shut—yet a splash upon the cheek,
Passed through the spillway, one little
Splash.

Mommy standing between the splash and
The hurricane. One little voice screaming
Silently about a hurricane in February.

The dam's broke. The screaming's louder.
The splashes fallen.

It's only February—and it's a pale yellow
Sky outside—and why are you crying?
1969

ON GIVING MY SON A NAME

March 22, 1966

Well, young Seamus, it seems your mother feels
You'll be a James or Jim to the kindergarten set.

Your grandfather—and mother's father—thinks
McGee will be Mac or Mike or something of the sort.

I've got news for them. Seamus McGee, it is. And
Seamus McGee it shall be.

I don't mean to be a boor—or bore—but
At your age, quite young—I doubt if

You'd care. So, here's my boring thought.
I mean pertinent. Or to the point. But let's
Get on with it.

When they try to call you James or Jim,
Let them. Once, I let them call me Dick. (!)

All the family thought it a gas. That means
Funny. I wonder if they understand.

Your father's father didn't. But then he had
A queer name for an Irishman. John.

But call yourself Seamus McGee. It will be hard
At first. And then worse. You may even have to fight one day.

And, be sure, you'll fight for bigger things, I suppose.
Or, you may think so, even. But listen:

Seamus, Sean, Delia, Deirdre and Moira.
Names.

John, Jack Jim And Bill.
Nice, eh?

You'll be more than a name, I hope, my son.
You'll be a man. And, as Burns says, And all that.

And when all the Irish folk are wearing the green
On Saint Pat's Day, they'll think of marching.

You think of Parnell, Danny O', Lamas, and,
Fitzpatrick, if you like.

When they whistle to the pipes,
You listen.

Stand straight, though, you should never hear the skirl of pipes unless you
stand straight.

Stand at the top of a great dark hill,
And look to the other great dark hills.

And listen to the skirl, then.
You won't whistle.

A lot of men died on hills like that.
Needlessly, foolishly. But for what

They called Freedom. The other day, in fact,
In Dublin, someone busted Nelson's beak.

Many laughed, called it:
Castrating a freak.

Some of us cheered.
Some laughed.

But when was the last time you—and
I think of you all grown and handsome—

Cheered and laughed and weren't a better man
For it? When?

So, when they called you James or Jim,

No matter.

You're Seamus McGee. Your father is Sean Kevin.

Your father's father was a man
From Mayo. Maybe you will never know

Him. But try.
Know us all.

Know yourself and know as much as you can,
But, most of all, know your name, my son.

It's not a big thing, a few letters
Strung here and there.

But when all the world's worrying about the
Marching and the band, you'll stand

On some dark hill looking at other dark hills.

You'll be a man, my son.
I'm sure of it. Even if they call you Jim
Or Jack or Bill.

And all that. Just remember
And all that.

New York City

March 22, 1966

These old Brownstones
Of Brooklyn's Borough
Stand in rows
And rows
And hold within
The silent lives
Of landlords, tenants,
And others I do not know;
And though they commune
With these lives withheld,
They do not speak to me.

1963

The Old Highway of Love

For Karen and Seamus
On Their Wedding Day
October 3, 1992

One day, not long ago,
We sat talking quietly
And soon the subject turned
To the ways it could or would have been
If only we had done it
This way—or that way.

And you said, "When you try to analyze
Why you took this turn or rejected that one
There doesn't seem to be much reason why—
I only know it makes me want to smile,
Sometimes makes me want to cry."

I said, "We come to this life with such hopes and dreams
And thought we knew it all, even when we knew

We didn't—and found it hard to stop and say
"Hold on, what's going on here?"

Now I see two young lovers,
Hand in hand, not for any reason,
Walking down a lane together
Without care—although I can see
Danger lurking in every tree.

I want to scream, "Look out!
Look out behind that tree. The one
That looks like all the others. Over there—
Under that rock, an evil cat is watching."

They see the wonder of it all—
How the sun glints in the rippled water,
How passion turns the leaves to red and gold,
How the sun warms their bones
And the night is delicious.

And now a large crescent moon grins down at them.
They see romance everywhere
While I see the coming darkness
And the first chill of winter.

Who will tell them about the headlong rush
Into the past that leaves you taking separate roads?
Who will tell them these hopes and dreams
Are mated with fears and scorn?

We thought our passion would sustain us
Through the short days of winter,
That our independence and newly won adulthood
Would somehow make us more fulfilled.

And now I sit in a hardback chair in the sun
Reflecting on two young lovers walking down a path
That turns into a beautiful country road
Through the trees and by the pond.

Do they know that passageway leads to a
Hard black twisting road that sports cars
Take in second gear at full revs until it plunges
Into the main highway of our lives.

And it all goes by so fast—
The loves that turned to brown,
The dreams covered with snow,
The hopes diminished by the solar equinox,
The time running out,
Running out, running out.

What have we here then that makes us
Part of the cosmic quilt,
Satisfied to spread out over the land,
Become a part of the great story?

The lesson of the moon

And the scarlet trees
Tell us one highway together
Is better than several brilliant paths alone.
That caring about what makes the other work
Is far more important than what we say.

Now you and I sit under the hollow moon
Waiting for the leaves to fall
Still anticipating the dawn, but
Girded against the cold.

Seamus Seeks Beauty in the Dawn –
An Early Morning Trip to the Jersey Shore

"Let us go, then, you and I ..."
To see the summer's dawning sky ...

I went to the shore to see the summer's dawn,
To smell the crab claws rich with oils
And roped paws bringing aliments and jaws
Police cars glaring coolly at the Griefs
Mourning the closed doors of the Inn,
Waiting the return of an ashen sky –

A canned life, opened and cooled.
A few asleep against the sky
Forgot their hot desires and cried,
Whimpered in sleep for their own…

Even though they say we were true
It never dawned on me or you.

I screeched with the gulls
A thousand screeching nights
Hoping someone would eventually cry:
"It's time to go."
And like the crowd accepting law
I entranced in sand to wait the dawn.
Silent salty smells came to see
The youth less pilgrimage – intensify
My youth less memories…
And now I smell their eyeing tones
With the age of a lonely sage
And wish to God I'd die.

It would dawn on you
If you only knew…

Then the Proctor of the dawn
Released the Goddess Morn to sate the skies
With glowing dawn; and I
Loath to rise, released the salty skies
To dwell in musty thighs of old

Smells and stinks of a million seamen's pukes,
And Griefs regurged with joy as I…
At the evening of night's sky;
And they and I, competing with nature's dyes,
Painted glory on the door…or on the floor.

They said we'd never be,
Not you, not they, not me.

New Jersey
1962

PONTE VEDRA

A lush, green, golfers challenge,
Today. I remember holding hands
On a sandy pebble road Walking

with Eva.

At the hill crest
A white horse with a white man
All dressed in white and arm banded
SP. Rifle in scabbard
Pistol on belt
Hand held high as if to stop A

convoy.

The black lady
I learned to love
Whispering to me
"Be quiet young man."

I now know Nazi subs
Attacked oil tankers off the coast
And sent up booby traps to

kill little boys. And 40

Years of racial discord to boot.

Waved on, the cleanup complete,
To play in the sand
Retreat to the shack we called
Beach house
On deserted dunes
For sandwiches and lemonade.

I have no memory of bombs blowing up.
Only lonely sand dunes
And a shack which one day was not there.
Hurricane, Eva said,
Which accomplished what dozens of Nazi
subs never could.

Ponte Vedra, today
A golf tournament
Beach houses, television crews, and golf
gods saying, "Better than most." And a
life better than most.

June 6, 1944
Sean Kevin Fitzpatrick

While you were away at war
I was driving my tricycle, eyes peeled for enemy planes
Above Naldo Street in Jacksonville, Florida
Waiting for da to come home From
Jacksonville Naval Air Station
Where he worked in the commissary.

While you were away at war
People loved and played and worked
At making more money, improving the old golf game Cutting the grass while
Grousing about gasoline stamps and shortages of Meat
and booze.

While you were away at war
Life dripped on amidst the gold stars on window sills
The blackout curtains unfurled at dusk,
The pith helmeted air raid wardens
Who every now and then looked at the sky-- All
to the big band tune of A String of Pearls.

While you were away at war
We slept in peace trying not to pee the bed,

And now that you sleep in peace
You should know that we do not study films
About our lives,
But we embrace yours.   June 6, 2010

Goldie Wants More

The girl always wants more.
More fun.
More walk.
More run.
More explore.
More sun and breeze.
More treats and cheese.
More rubs, more pats,
More brushes and combs.
More sleep. More love.
More life, more dreams.
The girl always wants more,
More anything, more everything.

Me, too, my little girl.
I want more, more than even you know.
I want more of everything you want.
More time to see you snooze More

time to love you.

Especially more...
Time.
But, little girl,
It is time and time does not give us more.
It never gives us more.
The life we had was grand.
But I am a man not a little girl.
And it is time to give you more than love.

I will always love the little girl Who
always wants more. RIP

I BEEN TO RENO
May 13, 2014

John Cash went there.

Said he been everywhere. I been to Reno

and remember it every year on this date.

43 times now.
I been everywhere man.
Paris. Vienna. Tokyo. Beijing.
London. Dublin. Edinburg. Toronto.
São Paulo. Antarctica. Torrance.
LA, San Fran and Wash DC.
But Reno was the one place
We could take snow cones in

the chapel.

And live happily ever after.

THE WAIT

He waits for his mama Under

the dining table

Eyes piercing the door
A groan here
A whine there
Now up and changing direction
To stare at the other door

Oh where oh where
Is my mama tonight I am so
tired of this old man I could
bite his fat hand.

February

We thought winter had had its fill of us.
We thought Jack Frost had gone his merry way.

We thought the sun seemed warmer through the windowpane.

We thought no more teeth gritting or freezing rain.

Perhaps a show of arms outside.

Perhaps a little snooze on the porch.

A warm afternoon ride.

Perhaps a warm breeze

Instead of a sneeze.

February,

Your name is mud at my house.

Or rather, slush!

1962

ORDINARY MOMENTS

Rushing to conclusion days

shorter, nights longer

No time to make dessert

Could it be ¾ million penguins?
Stinking up the horizon while rushing ashore at high speed
Or was it the sight of you clearing fences in hot pursuit of blue?

Perhaps crossing Arctic Circles on star lit nights or

singing badly in Lincoln Center?

Scaring me with you on horse to hounds,
Me, a Formula Ford, nose diving into volcanoes in an open cockpit?
Maybe the celebrity photogs at Cannes' festival
Pointing at us
Or living large at Hotel du Cap? More likely:
I remember hysterical laughter by the railroad tracks
Or lobbing old tennis balls while movie moguls chased us,
Fast forwarding video dramas while checking iPads, fighting over the Gazette
Or even just nodding by the fire.
These are the real gold nuggets
That protects us from cold cataclysm.

My love for you in ordinary moments

transcending the universe inhabiting

the starry skies.

April 15, 2012

For SEFBUSTER

Dancing with Sue-Ellen

Year after year
With thoughts

And desires and music All

the way.

The suspension of **real time**
Invaded our feet some twenty-eight years ago
Taking our awkward moves
Creating a dance that only we dance.
At first, we were like any others
Leaping into the pit
Specializing in old time rock,
Proud of Mary, sweating with Loui-I-Ehhh,
Stomping with the beat, even using the

rope-a-dope and bending our knees,

Hands Up! Bouncing to a Fender base.

These feats of athletic endeavor sometimes replaced
By joint hardening rubbings to Tennessee's waltz
Or even an erection created by Carpenters
Late at night, holding and patting and breathing deeply.

Time passing, intermingling dancing
With hard words, soft words, laughter and despair,

We searched for accommodation while raising
Three non-ballroom swingers, Caring for Zorba
and Star and Joe and Walter,
Who wore a bow tie in the barn and on the porch.

Our dance partners were called Charlie and Fred
And swung with us with an assortment of kitties
And gerbils and mice and bugs or even tarantulas,
None so deadly as the sweet insects we swatted
daily at Dancer and Blue Cross.

The music was sometimes discordant,
The moves without grace,
Feet smashing on feet,
Passions doused with vinegar
Salty with tears, Silent as Ice, Gulped
like wine.

But then again, sometimes the music
Overcame the the shuffle
Putting our bodies into a magnificent swirl.
Making two immense egos blend into one
Manic moving Being,
Feeling its way, first one, then two, now three
And ultimately four magnificent, magic feet

Dancing and Twirling and choreographed feet
Moving left and right, forward and back,
Arms entwined, unembarrassed, never crushing
Dancing, joyously moving, absolutely and unbelievably Knowing,
seasoned, experienced dancing feet.

The dance may have started years ago
But we have fooled them all, fooled ourselves, Those
who thought we'd never dance all the way,
Who may have thought we'd never keep the beat.

But the music is still playing,
The dance is still saying,
Hold me tight,
Rub my thigh,
Blow into my ears
We still have years
To bounce and run
Jitterbug and worldwide wrestling for fun, our
bond is only smoother and better done, we've
only just begun.

Walk On

My fine white steed moves out to the center ring

Strong muscles bulge in ways I can feel

His mane is clean and tied into tidy knots for the circus crowd

He pulls my muscles in strange and unusual ways

That unexpectedly hurt and feel good All

at the same time.

They clap and call him Indy, but I just smile and say,

"Walk On".

And I shall call him My Fine White Steed.

"Walk On"

My son will never hit the hanging curve, never field the bouncing punt

Never run to me and say, "I love you Papa".

He will never have all A's

Never be the class disrupter, never sling burgers at Mickey D's.

But today my son passed by me saying, "Walk

On".

And I called to my son with watery eyes.

"Walk On"

This boy has come a long way from dead silence and frothing resistance,

Fear trembling his lax frame. Living the life of wheel
chairs and baby food, no boyhood memories to take
to an early grave.
But this is a good day for fun and games.
I can still hear the first words he ever spoke.
We all looked at each other not daring to believe
That this silent child had finally cried out "Walk On".
Truly miracles happen on a horse's back
6-05-10

The gods must be... For Sue-Ellen on her birthday

My Greek grandfather, Papou,

Had words with me

About a ten-year-old girl
I adored

Who failed to show at my birthday party?

Once upon a time, the gods were in open revolt
On Mt. Olympus. Pissed because humans
Had all the fun. Those four legged, four armed, all
covered with hair creatures had the best time,
Laughing, scratching, shrieking and pleasuring 24/7.

So, Zeus gave the gods a lightning bolt and advised
"Use it wisely". The bolt cracked down on humans,
Splitting them, scattering parts
To the four corners of the earth.
And now the gods had their fun.

Those pathetic half humans began searching for
the other part.
Often finding the wrong half.
The gods laughed and laughed and laughed
Knowing what foolery was to come.

That's where you come in.
Thirty-two years of finding the wrong half
Creating mirth for the Mt Olympians

Shy and awkward and totally lost
In the wrong halves. That was me.

You, on the other hand, were
Beautiful, charming, romantic,
Practical, skillful, charismatic
 And warm as toast
On a cold winter's night.

My dopey looking, goof prone, farting
Spendthrift, bumbling and
Luke warm half self, somehow by chance,
Came crashing into
Yours.

That's where we come in.
Four legged, four armed;
All covered with hair, giggling and
snorting and Laughing and
Shrieking with joy.

On this monumental occasion
As we look back over time

And see so many wrong halves bouncing around,
We take joy in our whole.
Even if the gods must be pissed once again.
April 15, 2011

Lizzie

I love her because she always has Her
eyes on the next fence.
Her strange and weird sense of humor.

Her determined competence Seasoned

with strokes of brilliance.

Her love of horses.
Her love of dogs.
Her love of Ray.
Her love of mom.
Her love of me.
But most of all
Her voice and face and hair and Aura

of Sue.

Poetry on a Tauck bus
7/15/14

You can laugh all you want
And laugh we did.
Eric in his moose hat

    And cookies in his hand
All to the sounds of Nova Scotia
       The thump and bang of a cedilah band.
We laughed and gorged and
       Stalked the land.
 Laugh if you must
       But I hope you will trust
I did see the moose. The Moose
       The moose I did see.

But I never saw a whale.

The story is not told
There's a moral to the tale.
On the road with Eric
       Is better than seeing a whale.
Liscomb Lodge
Nova Scotia

For Suzanne Ellen

04152014

73

24/7

For ever and ever and a day
I will love you always
At night time when it is dark
At sunrise while you plan your day
Through winter's freeze, uplifting You

in the summer and fall.

Quiet your nervous shudder with my love, use

your peculiar anxiety to renew your hope

Because my love is with you always.

We cannot see what we have not seen.
We cannot hear what we have not heard.
But we know our love is a lasting bond
And this special day is just one 24/7 In

04/2014.

For Grace Beauchamp House

I have heard my name
Heard it called in the moist nighttime Michigan breeze.
Heard it above the hot dry Santa Anas of California.
Heard it in the classical music

Of the continent where you were born. And
most of all, I have heard it beyond the spray
Of my simple morning shower.

I have heard these callings with anxiousness---
A lingering panic from my childhood.
And I see my Mother's frantic eyes calling me.

The philosopher asks triumphantly: When are we mature?
A question that is answered very differently day from night.
Is it after first love? Or quiet sex?
A jungle war? A published work?
Grey hairs on the pillow?
A wistful look at a hollow moon?
Or is it just our weeping children telling us so?
All I know is that a part of me
   Stayed young –
Frightened by that haunting in the shower.

And now, Grace, you are leaving us.
Taking with you my wife's father.
Your memory kept him with us
   These twenty odd years
In his old flannel baseball shirt.
On a windswept golf links – Cold rain
falling into straight whiskey   And
keeping us warm.

He is going with you, Grace.
He is going with you.

This lovely old lady was not my flesh
But the blood that runs through my warm wife
And so, I learned to care for her over the years
Even while tripping over her faults and Over

Scotch and Christmas trees.

She loved you, Sue-Ellen. I could see

that despite all the fusses, And you,

Tony! You were a wonder.

I could never have lived up to that.
And the endless stories by the fire
Of Al and the radio man and A

baritone cop dispensing harmony

on a golf course at night.

I remember laughing with tears in my throat at

that last Hula-Lu.

Her memory was so damned perfect.
I thought so much of her was unused.
(Did she hear his cries in the shower?)
Judith and I may be only observers
But we know all of you so well
Our night fears are out
And we quickly pray there is so much more And

more yet.

I watch closely my strong quiet wife Going

about the adult things.

Will you hear the callings in the shower again?
An anxious cry. An isolated fear.
A chance to cry warm tears
And have them blend into the steaming shower.
(Remember when you were five
And the sky opened!)
You know so much more than I
Of passing, and so I ask you,
As our parents leave us,
Does that mean the cries will stop – and when?
The anxious eyes stop staring? The part

of us that thinks we'll always be Gasping

at the inescapable conclusion?

Perhaps those cries in the shower Are

gifts from our childhood –?

Like some Thanksgiving or Christmas memories.
A pungent pudding canned and on the shelf.
A song that keeps on coming
And drives the children to roll their eyes.
And then – suddenly – The staring

eyes of our children which

We confuse with those other unblinking ones.

Good night Grace. So much of you was left unused.
But that was your Plan.
And if you find your way with Al
And it's warm and comfortable there
Somehow try to let us know
With a warm burst of sunshine or another sign.
Good night dear Gracie from all of us.
You knew all along about those cries in the shower
That eventually leaves us and leaves us not happier but

better knowing how much we all have cared.

The Children's Choir

On one holy night
Riding to the Christmas concert
Your friend referred to me as agnostic And I

disagreed, "Not agnostic.

I believe in God
Just not the religions that chain God."
We grew silent in the presence of The Lord.
One other mild friend reminded us of the slaughter of small

children that bloody day.

I said,
"God, how could you?
How could you?" Nobody

answered.

Suzanne's morning song

The crow was angry
Pointing his beak at me
Cawing to high heaven
Enough to wake the dead.

But I was already awake
Watering the sunflowers
And sweeping the porch

From arrogant leaves and sticks.

The hardwood trees mixed
It up with the swaying pines
Roused into motion
By the northeast winds.

I think that crow was pointing
To the ground under the feeder
Where squirrels had run riot Scarfing

up the seed.

From the pail on the porch
I gathered the seeds and walked down

the hazardous slope to spread my

seed upon the ground.

One more caw as I headed
To the porch to retrieve
My coffee and my shmeared Bagel

with smoked lox.

The flutter of wings broke against
The breeze and six or was it eight Friendly crows had swooped

down to join the leader crow.

The crows pecked the ground
Slurping up the seeds
Gently mumbling among them
Filling their bellies.

After a while, they rose in unison
Peeling off into the swaying trees
Chasing the high clouds
Against the pale blue skies.

Now three squirrels crawled down
From the hardwoods with great caution Sucking
up any seeds the crows had missed Stocking up
for the imminent Fall.

This I observed before coffee
On a fine August morning Knowing
that scattering my seed Created
this glorious pageant.

Intimation of mortality

My balls
        sinking down

                        to water's edge
bigger, squishier
                        Hang Dog. Style.

My pee pee
        shrinking
to the size of a
pea.

My memory of friends, Romans, countrymen --
you know -- that guy who lived in -- that place Whatzisname?

But I know I hate that big son of a bitch.
2013